POINT BLANK

POINT BLANK

POEMS

ALAN KING

SILVER BIRCH PRESS
LOS ANGELES, CALIFORNIA

Published by Silver Birch Press

ISBN-13: 978-0997797220

ISBN-10: 0997797223

EMAIL: silver@silverbirchpress.com

WEB: silverbirchpress.com

BLOG: silverbirchpress.wordpress.com

MAILING ADDRESS:
Silver Birch Press
P.O. Box 29458
Los Angeles, CA 90029

COVER PHOTO: "The Man in the Fedora Hat" by Ewholo Jeroro, used by permission.

Author photo by Melanie Henderson.

For my wife, Tosin

CONTENTS

A man sooner or later discovers that he is the master-gardener of his soul, the director of his life.
—James Allen

POINT BLANK

HULK

Even the trees shudder
at the sight of me walking
the streets at night.

They tremble
as if I'm a defect.

Where I'm going,
I never know.
I get the urge and go.
That's freedom.
I forget that

because I'm black,
this late hour says
I'm up to no good,

says I'm a john
horny for Trouble
and her friends
working the block.

I forget that,
in America,
I'm not a man,
just one of a herd

the police are sent
to corral. Wind bends
the branches above me
as if I might swing from them.

White people look at me
and pretend they don't see
the breeding of slaves,

pretend not to know
why I hulk around
with anger and grief
swelling my biceps and thighs.

The other day, some rich
white guy rapes an unconscious
woman and gets probation.

Judge said he couldn't ruin
his life, but what about the herd
of us rounded up on suspicions,

as if our lives could be swept
into a crack in the floor.

Rage rattled the cage
of me.

All I remember was how
the trees shrank in my shadow.

ONE

SURE, YOU CAN ASK ME ABOUT HIP HOP
after Diane Burns

What's my street name?
No, I was never gunned down several times.
Yes, my name is Alan.
No, I never dove for cover behind parked cars
during a drive-by. No my life never flashed
before me like a hologram.
Oh? You think I look like 50 Cent?
My rap sheet only exists in the minds
of those who shutter when I ask for directions
or say, "excuse me," when they block the sidewalks.
No, I never had a record deal.
I did get invited to read at a poetry festival
in San Francisco. No, I'm not a studio gangster
brainstorming street beef scenarios with an agent,
or rhyming in the booth about imaginary riches.
I did write a poem once about mouth-shaped orchids
and their aromatic kisses.
I never took anyone's life, or made anyone
give mouth-to-barrel resuscitation
to a loaded weapon. I did almost cry the day
my niece was born.
Huh?
No, my battle scars came from climbing trees and
playing with fire.
Oh? You think I look like Olajuwon?
No, I never had dreams of ballin' in the NBA.
I dream all the time about one of my collections
winning the National Book Award.
I've never knuckled up with guys who hid
switchblades under their tongues.
Never been knocked unconscious,
left lying on a club floor.
Never bought a hoodie—wait—I did buy a hoodie once.
But I never bought rolling paper or reefer.
Never bought blunts, used box cutters or brass knuckles.
Never bought anything beginning with the letter "B"

17

except books, Blistex, and a bible—oh yeah—and Blow Pops.
I never inhaled marijuana shotguns blown
from Death's lips. Never wrote a love song to a firearm.
I did write a love poem for an aunt I lost to cancer.
I guess my presence intimidates. But
that wasn't me handcuffed, sitting on the curb,
while police searched my car.
Oh, you rap, too?
That nice, huh?
Oh, you got tattoos?
That street, huh?
I think I know you.
Weren't you in the movie *Jackass*?

WHERE THEY DO THAT AT?

I'm from salt fish for breakfast and
coconut bake steaming on counter tops,
from Byron Lee and The Dragonaires blaring

through basement speakers
when mom, my brother, my sister

and I come home from church. I'm from
card games in the backyard, from where
sunsets melt in Jack Daniel skies,

from where gunshot victims leak
mambo sauce on piss-infested streets.

Ask me where I live and I'll say
at the corner of Chuck Brown Lane
and Pharoahe Monch Ave, at the corner

of Roti and Rotisserie. I'm from after-
school fights at the ice cream truck,

from *don't let that green Lex*
with tinted windows find you wandering

the neighborhood late. I'm from
you lunchin' like... and *why you cised?*
from *don't lose a fight you ain't start*

and come home not expecting
another one. I'm from charcoal-scented

summers and whiskey-breath evenings
when the wind stumbles on its way
to the next bar-b-que, from okra and

callaloo bubbling in a pot, next to curry
goat and stewed ox tail. I'm from electric

slide lessons in the living room,
and dad snatching mom by the stove
to slow dance to The Whispers.

THIS GOOD

The truths are piled like hot wings
on a plate between us. You said you saw her
arm in arm with another man, strolling
past the bookstore,

Shame nowhere to call her out.
But I'm thinking of her lips and how her hair
falls like water.

If it feels this good getting used,
Bill Withers sings somewhere,
and we seem to be the only ones
in the crowded sports bar, listening to him
over cheers for Nigeria
in the World Cup.

Just keep on using me until you use me up,
a guy at the bar sings off-key before his friends laugh.
A singer's desperation drowns on a Friday
of beers and sports highlights.

Even if the truth came dripping
with garlic parmesan sauce or jerk seasoning,
wouldn't the heartburn be unavoidable?
We strain to hear the wounded crooner
everyone talks over.

I love pain, the way it drives us to distraction,
that simple response.

THE DELIGHTS

I thought you would be further along in your career.
But you got caught up by the outside forces.
—Dad

Why are your words piranhas?
Every morning I wake

is a banana split and mango sorbet.
Stray bullets, car bombs and suspicious
packages aren't so common here.

But there's my fiancée
and the space around us—
a grove of ginger and cinnamon-
flavored trees with leaves
tingling peppermint.

There is laughter.
Children chasing the ice cream
truck's chime.

It's not just knife wounds
and antiseptic.

There's the sound of a soccer ball
toed around, men grunting,
the cheering lawn chairs
and spectators gasping
as if their lives came down
to the final goal.

MATCH STICKS

Used to like matches—
wooden ones snoozing in box beds.
Never dad's stiff-paper nerves
ignited by backtalk,
like when he called me greedy
for not sharing a shake with my sister.
He was pinewood and sulfur
eager to cook my behind when I said,
I wonder where I get it from.

I blazed those adolescent years
when he said I had shit for brains
if I forgot to cut the grass
or didn't take out the trash.
I was a phosphorus-headed
boy who, when struck, torched everything
until my uncle told me careless fires
hurt innocent people.

I remember dad and I nearly
came to blows in the kitchen when he said
I wasted his money not graduating on time.
We were up in each other's faces,
then backed away when we heard mom crying,
the same reaction she had to the news:
a woman's body found
at home after a brush fire
chewed through her neighborhood,
leaving the charred remains
in its sooty footprints.

APPLES

I.

They hung in the yard, rotting
where fruit flies burrowed through
to make tenements out of Granny Smiths,

Empires and Honey Crisps.

Their sweet odors, the death
of them, veiled the evening. Holy corpses
riddled by hunger.

II.

At 16, I first saw bodies hanging
from nooses in a black and white postcard.
They hung with their eyes and privates

gouged out. The eyeless faces
watched people eating popcorn
and carrying children on their shoulders.

I WANTED BANANAS—

a bunch of them spooned body to body
like small yellow kayaks. So I missed

what you said about the war
in Libya. When you say Gaddafi,
I think of how they spoil
if they sit too long
on their wicker thrones.

We're in my car, listening
to WTOP. We passed a Spanish market
that calls what I love platanos.
Just saying plata-, my tongue snaps
like the slingshot's elastic strip,
hurling A's like stones.

You complain about the weak radio signal.
I could nod and punctuate your frustrations
with hums, as if I'm listening,
as if my head weren't full of Hunger's S.O.S.

I could pretend that the radio static
is annoying, as if the sizzling sound
it makes doesn't have me thinking
of sweet, chunky rhombus slices
frying in my mother's skillet,

or plantains boiled whole
with dasheen, dumplings
and potatoes to eat with salt fish
and coconut bake—

plates and plates
of large bananas, edible boomerangs,
nature's golden sugar-filled tusks,
the moon's waning frown
or waxing smile.

THE HOSTESS

She starts with oil. She simmers garlic
before adding curry. *Got to cook it real good,*
she says, *or else it'll mess up your stomach.*

Mom adds sugar to blacken the already dark
tint left on what pops and sizzles, what mixes
in the meat steaming in a bubbling bath of cumin,
turmeric and cayenne pepper.

Mom doesn't cook curry a lot, just on days
when dad comes home tired, when each day's
an opponent that leaves him bruised
like the bags of fruit he brings her.

One time mom wrapped her arms around his neck,
and dad said, *You only love me for my mangoes.*
They both laughed when mom said,
You gotta bring mangoes home more often.

He'd tell mom about the days
when his drill burnt out, when his truck got a flat
in the rain or didn't start,
when days seemed to plot against him,
as if he was a fighter
past his prime, unwilling to lie
down and throw the match.

And there's mom's curry
lingering in every room, opening the house
for his return. Dad enters her scent
that calls him to the kitchen, ready to put back
what the ring takes out of him.

WHAT MY FATHER SAID

It was the day I helped dad
clean out the shed, when Sly, Jay Bird
and Rashad darted to our fence
and, still panting, said
they needed a fullback
for our neighborhood league.

Back then, we'd snag any open turf.
Uniforms were street clothes
our parents bought the year before.

It was the Saturday of our fantasy
playoffs, two teams of teens
whose lack of coordination meant
the ball slipped through shaky hands
like our chances of making the school squad.

We dreamed of screaming stadiums,
cheerleaders boogying their beautiful bodies,
fans stomping the stands every time
one of us dove toward the end zone.
We were at that age when bragging rights
shined brighter than Super Bowl rings.

They asked if I could kick up the field with them.
I frizzled when dad said, *No, he's busy.*
That was the Saturday Mrs. Brown mulched
her rose bush and Mr. Graham set sprinklers
in a lawn that looked like AstroTurf.

That was the day I heard my boys
laugh two yards over, yelling *touch down*!

I went back inside the shed to help dad
move a spool of fat cables
before I saw black billows of smoke
over the shed before Mrs. Brown and

Mr. Graham called us out
to see a planted torch blazing
near the two struck matches.

I watched Sly and Jay Bird break
under the sun's interrogative gaze. I watched
angry fingers aim blame at one another.
I watched, grateful dad said no,
that accusations weren't huddled over me,
screaming: *Why you lying! You know
you set that fire!*

I lay in the grass, watching
my friends' parents whip them.
Rashad cried loud enough to scatter birds
from the lamp posts. That's
when I ran home.

DREAMS OF COMIC BOOK WOMEN
after Lyrae Van Clief-Stefanon

Give me everything I can touch:
What's round: What speeds
the blood: What raises the drawbridge:
What will fit on my tongue:
A hunger rising like thought bubbles.

The dreams are bright colors—
even at 16, waking to the promise
of Betty and Veronica, I wanted to be
Archie, caught between glossy mouths
like strawberry shortcakes.

Storm's battle suit swallowed her body
the way a boy gobbles a chocolate bar.
What I lick off my fingers, dreaming
of a perfect world where everything
can be touched without consequences.

I dream of sweet things: the tempting glaze
of a strudel, the moist center of an apple croissant;
or waking to Madame Hydra, Catwoman and Mystique
mistaking me for icing, a melting popsicle, ice cream
running down a waffle cone.

Give me the assassin, Elektra, in her Twizzler-
colored suit hanging as if someone attempted
to rip it off her. Let my appetite for sweets keep me
dreaming through the wars and unemployment.
Let me go on like Ulysses' men, wandering—
never dreaming of home.

SWARM

In a mob of school kids,
two boys shove each other
before they're on the ground.

They jab at air and grass,
missing the jaw, cheek and eye.
A girl standing at the edge
screams at the boy
straddling his opponent.

Leave him alone.
This won't make me like you.

I watch from my car
across the street
after cruising through an old 'hood,
two decades removed
from my childhood.

And yet this gust spirals
the pinwheel of memory,
whirling me back to third grade,

when I obsessed over Tia Jones
the way my friends swarmed
the ice cream truck for grape Pixy Stix.

She was a sixth grader, who mistook
my lamppost legs and power line arms
for a fifth grader.

She was as old as the boys
throwing grass in each other's hair,
rolling around in a kind of awkward
tango towards manhood.

Watching the chubby kid

overpower his skinny enemy,
I'm reminded of Darnell,
an older boy too short for Tia.

That's when I wonder
if Insecurity's the biggest instigator.
The one constantly egging you on
to prove yourself,
like that day Darnell kept asking,
Why you so stupid?

It was the day I gave Tia
a Valentine's card I made
with construction paper
and magic markers.

She kissed my cheek,
her lips flipped the switch
to the streetlights inside me.

Why you so stupid? Darnell said.
He shoved me. *You so stupid
you don't even speak.*

Tia's fingers locked with mine,
Let's get out of here.

I didn't speak when he snatched her card
and tore it, when I unzipped my bag,
pulled out cleats, and smacked him.

I was a nest of wasps.
Each cleat stung him
over and over.

A woman's yell calls me back
across the street. It's the neighbor
on her front porch, wearing
a blue tattered housecoat
and floppy pink slippers.

31

She holds up her phone,
and the crowd scatters,
Y'all need to stop! I got police on the line!

I wish I had someone like her
to save me from myself
before Darnell's tears streaked
over welts big as bee stings.
Tia nowhere in sight.

BLOOM

When my doctor saw
a lump on my groin
and said, *It might be cancerous,*
what I took for granted
taunted me: mom laughing
at dad's jokes, her callaloo
with crab legs, my 3-year-old
niece's explorations starting with
Uncle, what's that?

Wasn't I too young,
too green for Death to pick me?
The thought of meeting Him so soon
made my life a smorgasbord
of untasted desires.

I wanted to bathe
on a Bali beach, backpack through
a Costa Rican rainforest, nibble on
a Moroccan vender's
steamed lamb tangine.

I wanted a wife so fine
her hairpin curves
send my heart skidding.

I was a tree surgeon
snipping at fungus on bark.
What bloomed made me
a mushroom in a field of daisies.

My mind became a house
I tried to get in order:
what I didn't know about myself
were unlabeled boxes
waiting to be hoisted
into a delivery van

along with everything else
I ran my hands along,
as if explanations
were in the hard edges
of perishable things.

THE LISTENER
for Marilyn King, "Mops" (1949-2009)

A woman in the next aisle
laughs among the milk
and orange juice.

Laughter stops the words in her throat,
so no matter what, they won't finish the joke.
She laughs like my Aunt "Mops,"

the one who was ready to drive
from DC to Baltimore to scorch my boss
with her fire-bottle words
when I told her what I made as a reporter
forced to work weekends.

She got her nickname, "Mops,"
from the Mopsy biscuits she loved
as a girl back in Trinidad.

Every Friday, I'd snatch a stack
of newspapers from my job and race down
to her house where the aromas
of pound cake and curry
fought each other like siblings.

I'd drop off a few copies at her salon.
She'd smile, *See how my nephew all ova'
the front page, so!* She'd keep a paper
to read my articles on city council corruption
and displaced East Baltimore residents
before she fell asleep.

If I was stressed from work, she'd always say,
Them can't play sailor and 'fraid powder.

When she died from cancer,
I thought I lost her forever.

But she's an aisle over,
laughing
behind the spice shelf.

BEHOLDEN

Another day lands
like a rolled-up newspaper
smacking the front porch.

And I'm glad to wake
with my soul like a row
of chandeliers
lighting my inner cathedral—

food globs passing
like a collection plate
from stomach to liver, kidneys
and intestines. Nutrition—
the body's tithes and offering.

Knowing this, my wife's smile
is a billboard for better living.
I once asked for dessert,
and she slid me Fuji apple slices
and plump red grapes,

sad consolations for the German
chocolate cake and sweet potato pie
that thrilled my blood's locomotive

until I remember two years ago,
watching my parents prick themselves,
checking their blood, shooting
insulin when their sugar spiked.

I so sweet, Dad once said. *I spoil!*
Mom's laugh swallowed my chuckles.

It wasn't funny the following year,
when I sweated my lab test,
wondering if glucose got me,
if I'd lose my limbs and digits

to its gluttony. Or worse.
But I'm still intact, laying in bed
while first light pours over my wife
in the bathroom mirror, over
our cockatiels fussing for feed.

And I'm happy I have those sounds
for the sun's slow climb in the horizon,
grateful that nothing trips my inner
fire bells and strobes,
that another day thuds
against the waking door.

Two

THE WATCH

Like a magician's assistant
in a prop box, my watch
vanished from a gym locker.

Its Timex analog glowing hands
sliced at each other the way
dad and I crossed words,
when I started smelling my musk
and outgrew the lectures.

It kept kicking despite the gang
of years scuffing its silver band,
scratching its face.

The *tick, tick, tick* of seconds throbbing
the metronome of persistence
that woke my Trini parents, pushing them
to provide for three kids
despite the electricians at dad's job
and the secretaries at mom's
who joked about foreigners.

It was dad's timepiece, a lesson
in patience the minutes and hours taught me,
swinging their bright
sabers in a lazy light battle.

It was the watch he sported
when he took mom to the movies.
His English Leather cologne,
splashed across it, a fragrant stain
that followed me when he passed it on.

The absence of it
still popping up years later
haunting the replacements.

DISTURBANCE

A shirtless man with rags for pants walks up to a car
and asks for change. He wipes his sweaty
stomach with a rolled up jersey. Around him,
are the sounds of police sirens, the rush of traffic

at the intersection. You imagine he might be
a war veteran because of the army fatigue pants.
The remaining hair gathers around a bald spot
on his head the way a forest surrounds

a clearing you played in long ago. You, playing kickball
with your friends, were frightened then by the voices
you heard from beyond the trees. You are eight
or nine in a white tee and khaki shorts, watching

from a McDonalds, slurping your Sprite through a skinny
straw, wondering what the driver said to make the vet spit
on the car, jump on the hood, and start stomping
the windshield. That's when the world becomes scarier,

when you discover the darkness that lurks outside
your "Happy Meal" life, when you learn danger
needs very little to combust and consume whatever's
in its way. Customers run into McDonalds, and you

almost hear what leaves the spittle-laced mouth
of the beggar. People inside press to the windows like salt
against the sides of a shaker you pick up and fool with
out of nervousness. The crowd forms a semi-circle

around the driver locked in his car on his cell, the beggar
punching the glass and kicking the fender. You go back
to the clearing, where you imagine cardinals pecking grubs
before the sounds of a larger animal send them scattering.

SLIPPERY

The need for change bulldozed a road down the center
of my mind.
                    —Maya Angelou

Hey man, I know I did some triflin' stuff back in the day.
I'm not that cat anymore.
                    —Rahim

That Facebook message pops up
after a decade of silence.
It's Rahim.

Most folks called him "Droopy" because
every time he blazed blunts
his eyes were shade-drawn windows.

Others called him Dark Knife—
the emcee assassin, collecting
microphone casualties.

I knew him as Rahim, the poet
who called every brotha "king"
and greeted their women, *Peace queen!*

Let the guys get distracted,
Rah was Nagchampa smoke
in their women's afro, her black dashiki
and tight jeans.

He was Terrance to his mom
before he joined the army.

I made him mad once, joking
he had more aliases than witness protection.
Who you owe money? I snapped. *Whatchu hidin'?*

He's married now and wants to know
if we can hang out again.

Just the other day,
working a metal cart through
the baking aisle, I spotted a woman
who put icicles in my blood.

She was standing near the spices
and herbs, wearing jeans
and a cayenne-color blouse.

But she wasn't who I thought
she was. Her paprika-bright lips and
adobo tan skin brought back a moment
nearly a decade ago.

She resembled that woman
Rah hooked me up with
at a bar in Manhattan.

Her name was Catalonia
like the itch on Spain's head
that holds Barcelona's sapphire sunsets.

Cat's eyes were that blue. Her hair
made me think of a magic fountain—
its cascade of curls lit by
pink, blue, and green laser lights.

Three months later, we were bobbing
our heads to Talib Kweli and Dead Prez
at a live show in Central Park.

I was planning another trip up there
before Rah swooped on her
when his other plans fell through.

He boasted about his fling
with her—how her mouth played over

his tender parts, how she was a bright horn
whose notes he jazzed out.

He was the Trojan horse that
overran those who trusted him
before they ran him out of the city.

He was a used Lifestyle
lying on a sidewalk, a drooping Magnum
in a stairwell, lubricant oozing
from its wrapper.

I could hate him
if time wasn't a bulldozer,

if forgiveness wasn't a road paved
down the center of my mind.

And yet my mouse lingers
over his message, wondering
whether to respond
or close him out.

No Substitute

Yes, sweetheart, I stopped guzzling Sierra Mist.
And I no longer eye a sausage and pepperoni pizza
as if it was a Turkish spice market, as if grease
and cheese mimicked a Hawaiian sunset.

Under heat lamps, the glazed toppings
tempt my tongue. OK, OK, of course I know
my veins and arteries are the blood's highways
and interstates, that too much of what I love
will slow traffic like an accident.

Those spicy wings mobbed with fries,
the strawberry shortcake, and that apple pie
with syrup and ice cream will be the death of me.

But see my point—walnuts and
dried fruit are no substitute. Tell me, baby,
should we starve desire?

The Brute

He called you Alex.
He's the supervisor who asked you
to read poems at a holiday party, then said,
Don't get too Black with it. Your name is Alan.

He was light enough to pass,
had a gray high-top fade
and, on Fridays, wore his leather
"Road Dawgs" jacket.

You imagined him scorching streets
with his middle-aged motorcycle crew
posting up in parking lots,
chilling on their choppers

until a better idea rode by
in her cherry red Camry—
sunroof tilted, windows down,
Dr. Dre's *Chronic 2001* blasting.

You remembered the "hard boys"
from high school with cigarette burns
and homemade tattoos
stung into their biceps.

Yo, I got a knuckle sandwich,
they'd yell to no one in particular.
And you can get that with fries, too, money.

You wondered if they grew up
to be men like your boss—
riding their authority like Harleys,
revving at subordinates
scrambling out their way?

You once had to soften up
one of those hard boys.

Your hair ain't natural, he said.
Why you rockin' an S-curl, homie?!

That's why your 'fro so thirsty, you came back,
when you comb it, it sound like Velcro.
Everyone laughed.

And here it was your turn again
when the boss told you
it was a mistake to study journalism.
*Boy, you should've majored in something
that makes money.*

Thanks, you said, *but I didn't ask you.*
He grimaced and the workers smiled,
their triumph shifting the air.

You grew 10 feet, staring him down,
knowing he wanted to deck you
before his bad hip and knee screws
told him not to knuckle samba with a 22-year-old—
too broke to move out his parents' house,
a young brother desperate
for a clown to punch.

And here he was, every bit
the badass he thought he was
'til Trouble rolled on 'em.

BOUND

On the bus in rush hour, he enters
with the brim of his baseball cap
over his left ear, where a snubbed out
Black & Mild sits like an aromatic
marker with its black tip exposed.

You checked the weather today.
Cloudy skies with a chance of rain.
Your boss called you into his office,
talked about the economy and running
a struggling paper, how he's got to let you go.

Think of it as a paid vacation,
he said. You look up at the guy
with the Yankees cap and phone to his ear.
I'm on my way, babe.

His smile says his destination
is a garden hidden in a labyrinth,
where the sun slides its iridescent tongue
over a tamarind-colored woman,
oiling her skin while she sleeps
among orchids and birds of paradise.

You imagine that garden
on the other side of your front door,
where you'll open like morning glories
when your wife
descends on you like dew.

AT THE HIGH POINT

The whacking headboard
and squealing mattress means
your twenty-something-year-old
neighbors, above you, are at it again.

You hear galloping bed legs
and imagine lovers in a mad dash
to pop up at their destination,
as if the course wasn't meant to slow them
along its turquoise coast.

Weren't you naïve once, thinking
all there was to keeping a woman
was breaking the last man's record
while she cried out,
then kissed you afterwards?

That's when you were young enough
to see the climax as a finish line
you bolted across before collapsing,
breathless and disoriented,
like the couple upstairs
whose sounds slide down
to you and your sleeping wife—

who, earlier, vacuumed the living room
while you streamed movies—
scanning the action category—
munching popcorn,
swigging a ginger beer.

Now you watch her stir
under the sheets, knowing—
after years of complaints
about your dirty dishes
crowding the sink and clothes piling
a couch arm—your life together

is far from its climax.
Her sleeping smile,
a bright song in its slow rise
to crescendo.

UPTOWN

after Tony Hoagland

A bee that sounds like an electric razor says something
to a bee that sounds like a punctured muffler.

The sun interrogates the grass that sambas when the wind
pulls its imaginary strings. Inside an apartment,

a cockatiel throws its song like an alley-oop

through an open window to a bird with a cry
like a dot matrix printer. Around here, flowers

are musk merchants enticing with their scents.
Trees hover like street ballers posing

for Sports Illustrated. No. They're emcees
kicking chlorophyll rhymes

while b-boy weeds uprock concrete around a strip mall
of liquor stores and carry-outs.

In all of this, Pixy Stix powder colors the sunset tongues
of young mothers, wheeling their strollers

down the avenue. Their bodies tense as bluebell buds
to the ultraviolet stares of brothas.

Somewhere, sirens wail like horn-mouth babies,
like Miles at the Five Spot. Crushed
berries mark the street like chalk-outs.

In all of this, bodies fall like branches
blown away by hollow-tip winds while dead leaves

and petals litter cracked sidewalks
like shell casings.

THE LAST NIGHT AT THE CLUB

Pepper spray swarmed Jerry's eyes,
police K-9s sniffed for Brian in a grove of denim
and bare legs. A blood trail snaked its way
through Timbs and stilettos, past the butterfly knife
on a flower pattern in the ceramic tile.

Biggie pumped through gaping speakers. The club air
was kerosene. The wrong look, was a struck match.
You and your boys didn't go inside at the same time.

"It's never alright to let anyone see how deep you roll,"
Chuck once told you. That's why you called him
"Young Sun Tzu," the smallest of the crew.

He made avoiding beat downs an art.
You remember, in college, when the threat
for looking at a jock's girlfriend stood over him

before Chuck faked a love letter between the jock
and a teammate, posted copies around school,
and made out with the girl
while her boyfriend fought the fellas.

Twenty bucks got you in the club and spot on the wall,
while a woman's gyrating thighs
punctuated your pulse with exclamations.

Your heart was a woodpecker, hammering your chest
when her shake found you. Her scent
like honeysuckle you and your friends once ran
to collect during recess.

You remember undoing the silk bells, tangled
in a wire length fence
before an angry man shooed you away
from his yard.

That night, your brothas didn't back down
when the woman's boyfriend threw his palms
into your chest

before Jerry tagged his jaw, before
a blade's glinting light butterflied Brian's forearm
and stomach, before the opposing crew swelled in error,

and, just when they thought
they had your ass,
Chuck signaled for the boys
to knuckle up.

BOOTH SEAT

2009

I'm in a booth where I chomp a chili burger
& slide fries through ketchup
& mustard: Stevie Wonder's "Sir Duke" on the jukebox,
walls covered by signed photos—
Denzel Washington, Bill Cosby, President Obama—
the big screen TVs over humming iced tea
machines & chilled bins of sliced tomatoes,
lettuce & onions. I sit there the way I did
five years before, when I showed a woman the city
on my birthday. I remember Tim, the short-order cook,
saw me waiting, then saw my date
& nodded: *Go sit with your lady, homie.*
I'll bring your order out.

He's a ghost now—carjacked and shot,
scooping a friend from the subway
to work on a rap CD.
That year, Death tore through the city
in his souped-up ride, racking up body counts
on his odometer. That year, the other cooks suffered
quietly—Stevie singing loud as though his sounds
could drown out Tim's jokes or his rap lyrics
replaying in their heads
while flipping burgers & slicing half-smokes.

That was the year Ben, who stayed open
through the '68 riots, closed early.
I'm sitting here, staring at Tim's photo
on the wall next to the dessert case.
I remember that date and the slice
of chocolate cake I bought her. She picked at it
until it disappeared the way she did
three days afterwards, with no explanation.
I see my reflection frowning in the mirror—wondering
if I could tie on an apron in Ben's where
every day a ghost stares back from a taped photo

or like the cooks, reminisce and laugh
whenever Tim started on the mama jokes.

THREE

SUGAR SHACK
for Ernie Barnes

Looking at "Sugar Shack" by Ernie Barnes
in early November, I stared at women
whose backsides curved like hooks. The men,

snapping their fingers and stretching skinny
limbs, were a school of fish swimming
among anglers. They existed in a world of oil

and canvas. They danced as if it was the 1970s,
the decade my parents emigrated here from Trinidad.
U.S. soldiers were already dying in South Vietnam's

rice paddies. My mom wore a white dress
with a train. A rice cloud followed my parents
from the altar to church doors. I was

looking at "Sugar Shack," staring at women
swing and slide, as if a flame slithered
down their spines. I walked through the frame

of the painting where Marvin Gaye's banner
hung from the ceiling. I crossed the frame
like the threshold of a house. Marvin Gaye's singing

through cracks and pops on a worn 45.
A woman who sounds like my mom
laughs at a shadow shaped like my father,

then bedsprings moan. Marvin's serenade
cracks and pops. The 45 moans like the lovers
in the next room, giggling while they made me.

I was looking at "Sugar Shack," staring at women
whose jelly-rhythms turned men into toddlers
learning the shapes of things, having forgotten

their names. I walked through the frame
and saw my parents single, staring at each other
through the crowd.

THE CHAMP
for Andrew and Anicia

My sister's daughter says *O-boo* instead
of uncle, and says my brother's name first:

O-boo Drew!, O-boo Drew! And the look
she gives me, when I try to get her to say
O-boo Al, is the silver screen
after theater lights are back on.

I'm a sad production assistant
at a premiere, looking for my name
in the credits, long after the crowd
has left the lobby.

And something I hadn't seen since
we were kids sweeps across my brother's face
the way it did when he took the steering wheel
as the daredevil stuntman in the action
flick called *Those Teenage Years.*

I remember that Christmas Eve his car leaped
from the beltway through a column of trees.
That night, I waited to bail him out
after an officer found him
drunk in his battered coup.

He quit school for the Air Force,
and I can still hear dad yelling:
*I didn't bring you into this world to be a pawn
on a battle field!*

Mom shook her head, wondering
what he had to prove. I couldn't understand
why my brother's Tae Kwon Do trophies
and black belt weren't enough.

I know we're always given a chance

to do something brave, even it means
him whisking our terrified niece out the way
of the villainous vacuum cleaner.

Now, Anicia's laughing and clapping
for her uncle who's won the Oscar
of her affection. She's chanting:
O-boo Drew! O-boo Drew!

X-MEN
for Truth Thomas and the students at Homewood

Drew's battling in the Danger Cave.
His rhymes are retracting metal claws he swings
at holograms that lunge at him.
Disappointments are collapsing walls
he back flips to avoid. Sometimes I wonder
if you have to be an acrobat
to survive America. The way she treats me
I might as well have an X-gene.
Just the other day, when a police cruiser
followed me for several blocks,
my heart was a speaker with the bass
turned up. Sweat beads popped out
like the heads of nosy neighbors.
Like the students at Homewood,
I wish I could teleport out of those moments
or shape-shift to a human.
Truth says they need what we bring them
every Tuesday, and I remember his ruby quartz
battle visor glowing when he emits his wisdom:
This world is fucked up, but it don't have to stay that way.
The optic blast in their minds has incandescent stanzas
shooting out of Bryan when he kicks his verse,
while Amelia levitates verses
in the telekinetic air.

BUGGED

Clicks turn my blood into juice startled
by the blender's blade.

Clicking on my BlackBerry
makes me think it's been co-opted.
When I tell my friends, they say I read
too many books about Black Panthers,
that I've seen too many episodes of *The Wire*.

I'm on the phone with my brother
who calls for weed, and think
of swat teams coming out of nowhere.

Clicking sounds make us jump to native speak.
You got that spinach, bruh, he says. I tell him,
You know I gotchu on them green Skittles.

I'm rockin' a hands-free earpiece.
Clicks give me headaches, make me
sorry I brushed off warnings
about phone signals causing cancer.

But what kills the black man quicker
patrols in government-issued rides.

My phone's got to be a snitch.
The other day, I called my boy and we spoke
about government resistance around the world
until we heard clicking.

Yo! Why don't you roll through? he said.
It ain't safe to be on these phones.

Click, click. There it goes again.
Any minute now
they'll storm that door.

"...PLAY SOME LUTHER"

How much you owe Leon?
What he say would happen
if you don't have his bread Friday?

Today Wednesday. All you gotta do
is keep the car running, make sure
you here when we come out.

You ain't gotta worry
about bank cameras or that old ass
security guard itching to re-live
his hot-headed days on the force.

You don't gotta watch
the slick cashier
tripping over the alarm.

No exploding paint dye
in the money sack. All you gotta do is
chill. Play some Luther, let his hook
school you in all this:

Never too much, never too much.

Think of that feeling tossin'
Leon a crisp loaf. No more watchin'
every car creepin'
down your block.

No more wondering if all them
hard eyes around you is Leon's boys,
waiting on his word to bounce you
like a bad check.

Everything can change today.
All you gotta do is keep that engine warm.
See what I'm sayin'?

GETTING A LITTLE ON THE SIDE

The tracking device on her car
says he's at the right place. Most days
he listens to what bugged phones tell him
or he's a screen name lurking in chat rooms,

but today he's across the street
from the Thai restaurant, waiting on a woman
who hasn't touched her husband
in over a year.

He's in an '85 Corolla. Stereo volume
down. She left her husband a note
on the fridge: *I won't be home until late.*

The private eye's out to catch a woman
whose husband thinks her perfume's
too strong for someone bending
figures all day at a firm downtown.

The brothers passing by
bob their heads
to Chuck Brown's "Bustin' Loose"
that shakes a nearby battered car.

On the passenger seat,
an envelope of crisp dollar bills.
All he has to do is get her
in his viewer and start shooting.

There's an outdoor bar,
screens yelling sports,
Grizzlies shut down the Spurs
in the playoffs.

Then, like a hiccup, she pops up
in a green dress and black leggings
that hug her supermodel body.

Her shoulder-length brown locks
bounce to her heel rhythm
on the concrete runway.
She doesn't care if she's caught.
She feels justified.

Wasn't her husband too busy
to spend time with her?
Weren't her suspicions nudged
by the toothpaste fresh on his breath,
or his soap scent strong
after a day of power lunches
and evening cocktails?

Her husband says she told him
not to visit her at work anymore.

She's with a guy, whose goatee
and shades say he's a playboy.
But they could be the handholding couple
the private eye saw earlier, strolling past
Smoothie Hut and Potbelly Sandwich Shop.

The detective lifts his Nikon
to the gaping window
and remembers when someone
caught his wife stepping out.

He almost blurs the shot
when he spots the woman's Trojan
horse tattoo on her left shoulder,
the same one his ex-wife had
on her right ankle.

MR. ON-TIME

Every ex-boyfriend hated me
when I was single. His used-to-be
got to know me as Mr. On-Time-
To-Pick-Her-Up.

Even in a zip-up cardigan
and dress jeans, I show up
like a sky blue Bentley belting out
Peabo Bryson's "Feel the Fire."

I was that smile on her face
over Thai basil eggplant and rice
when I said her kiss was a cozy lounge
with a fireplace going and Spacek's "Thursday"
spooling through wall speakers.

She kissed like that, enough
to buzz a lesser man's brain
bright as a heat bulb.

She had those curves that,
if you weren't ready, made you
a car on a winding road at night
with busted headlights.

Her smile was a condo on a quiet side
of town—a dim living room with a coffee table
holding up a scrabble board, two glasses
and a bottle of Irish Cream.

The song of lost love is Regret
whimpering in upturned hands,
begging for a road on which to cruise back
into her good graces.

But I'm her Dark Knight, now.
My symbol glows in the ether

when Need calls me from my hideout.
I show up like a chauffeured Lincoln, ready
to whisk her away from disappointments.

I'm her speed dial genie dissolving
in a poof, reappearing with
the ground cumin and coriander
that makes her Malaysian dish perfect.

His lapse in judgment was
an open window I swung through.
My time like a wad of money
burning to be spent.

Freeze

A man sits handcuffed on the curb
while his trunk and back seat are searched.

You watch from across the street,
heading to your car. His woman
was making a Malaysian chicken dish, sent him
to pick up coconut milk and curry.

It's night. The sound of car tires
on wet street makes you think of paper
torn slow in long strips.

The officers, thorough in their search,
remind you of thieves you once saw.

You couldn't say what you felt,
watching them take their time,
as if instead of searching for money and CDs
they were detailing the interior.

The man is every WANTED poster
you saw on TV, in the papers,
in post offices.

He is that night years ago.
When you followed your mom to return a rental,
and lost her in traffic, when the red and blue
flashes made you
a cornered cat.

You tense up when that moment
on the street gets just as close. Your keys
in one hand, sorbet and cookies in the other.

At the sight of what flashed in his mirror,
he knew he was tagged in a game older
than Jim Crow. Tonight, the sirens

and police lights say, *Get off the street*
unless you want trouble, too.

But the wind shoves you down the block,
muscling you back to your car
and to everything you love. You think
of the handcuffed brother
and his woman growing restless,
trying not to worry.

INNER WEATHER

Don't you know
when you're gone,
rain fills sink holes.

Thunder startles the silence.
The weather vane
is a confused compass
in a schizophrenic storm.

I wonder if I'm destined
to wait forever.
Your smile is a hot spring
bubbling in the Colorado mountains,
a bright villa illuminating
the Austria alps.

It's a star, arriving, blazing
despite the blizzard. The light of it
glittering ice patches cracking
under a feverish weight.

THE ANGEL SPEAKS WITH
THE *NEW YORK TIMES*

What, the Garden of Eden?
That's what you think it's like up there?

Back home, I'm a souljah,
posted along the perimeter of heaven.
You'd think afta a millennial
of battlin' dark forces, we'd get a parade,
be allowed to get a lil' action
from da groupies.

We can't leave you mortals alone
for a second, without the rogue ones
tryna' kill each otha'. This one's mad
at that one for somethin' that happened
before they were born.

This one's darka' than that one,
so that one's gotta conquer this one.
Now, I gotta wipe da milk
off their mouths.

But I ain't complainin'. It's betta than
standing around, laughin' at God's jokes,
pamperin' and praisin' Him all da time.

This must be where you end up
when He catches you dreamin'
of busty Victoria Secret Angels.
Now I'm posin' as a mortal
undercover, waitin' for Lucifer
and his henchmen to pop up.

Rookies? They get distracted,
and there's a lotta' that.
My mortal body fights tha circus
that masquerades as news.

It's enough to make a rookie blow his cover,
convinced he seen tha devil already.

There's a pro-lifa' supportin' tha death penalty.
Oh Snap! There's Mr. Fam'ly Values makin' it rain
at strip clubs. Tha "unbiased" media's a button
on the corporate lapel.

Oh, I'ma be here a minute.
Gotta reach those knuckleheads.
Gotta' give it to Mr. Big Horns.
He puts on a helluva show.

Peter Parker Contemplates
the Election Results
after midterm 2010

Here, the weather's never
what it says it is. And shine
as she might, Mary Jane's presence

tonight won't combat
the absence of hope.

Even now, wishing Uncle Ben
were here to explain what happened,
a rogue gallery of villains

overtook the House.
Even Captain America's delusional,

talking about knowing freedom
and fighting for it while those
against the takeover know only compromise.

My country will never be Aunt May,
whose chocolate chip oatmeal cookies

and childhood stories
of chasing Brooklyn's bad boys
before meeting Uncle Ben,

made anyone at home.
Where do I seek comfort now

when even Spider Man
seems outmatched by what's already
airborne and cackling?

FOUR

Exodus

They might be the weary Israelites
camping around the Tabernacle,

having wandered into the desert.
Night blind as the cripple outside
the gates of a temple called Beautiful.

A whiskey-ripened man
known as Moses mumbles

what passes for tongues.
The wind works
a Christmas display of bells

like tambourines.
The true sermon

happens every twilight
on Saturdays,
when Chubby Eddie jumps up

from the curb outside
Tick Tock Liquors, screaming:

Lawd, this world's too ugly for sober eyes.
All those souls outside of paradise,
anticipating the other side.

THE EXCHANGE
for Tos

Because the day's threaded through hours
the way a skewer's threaded through meat,
because I needed your whispers
wafting through the cove of my ears,
I look for you in a blur of blue jays.

I listen for you in the sounds of trees
brushing their crowns against a cold wind
hard and flat as cymbals.

I descend the stairs to touch your face.
Give me your skewered hours, the meat
and vegetables of your days. My mouth—
a welcome below a waiting threshold.

Hours roasting away. Your locks coil
like coral, your eyes bright as dawn above water.
I give you my mouth, flying to the light
in your dusk-colored skin. Your laugh—
the wind returning from Victoria Island.

Let me be the Atlantic, and you
a Lagos shoreline that hugs it.
Give me your face snug
against my neck. Here.
Place your heel in my hand.
I am your glass slipper.

BRINK

In a restaurant, a server became
a stone when asked for a refill
on Sprite. Closing my eyes,
my nose remembers

the seduction of turmeric and
mustard seed, my tongue tingles
of cayenne and rice flavored
with cumin and mint leaves.

In that restaurant where I won't return,
a server brought me half a glass of Sprite.
The sound of glass slammed on a table
made me think of gavels.

Everyone knows black people
demand high but tip low, a friend says.
The owner's expression dark as a judge's robe.
I closed my eyes and I thought

of a jury with everyone like him.
What my nose and mouth
once knew disappears. I could be
at my aunt's table in Trinidad,

devouring dumplings and lentil soup,
guzzling a cherry Kola Champagne—
far away from this place, where
my dark skin makes me a cockroach
in the kitchen, a grease spot on
a white wall, a rat in the dining room.

THE VIGILANTE
for the end of the world

When the world ends,
I'll run shirtless
through rich neighborhoods,
stoning the large windows,
with no blinds, showing off:

their Chinese porcelain vases,
their top shelf whiskey, *their* trays
of edible gold cupcakes.

My stacked bills and empty wallet,
the way they watch me in *their* stores
as if I'm a roach on a chandelier,
how they buy their way into everything,
and blame everyone else for their problems
numb me to empathy.

I will be a big wind crashing
through those shattered chasms,
looking for the Georgetown doctor
who screamed at my wife for saying,
I don't think I need surgery.

I'm the doctor! he spat.
I went to school for this!

I will be a crazed Rottweiler
Fury unleashes on him, a Rottweiler
with bear trap jaws and teeth
eager to snap his bones—
the pain a blooming reminder
that he's no god.

Neither is the fast-talking surgeon
who scoffed when my wife said
her shoulder didn't fully heal.

Your physical therapist is an idiot!
She's not relevant anyway.

When the world ends,
I'll be a cannon Karma fires
at Arrogance, the floodwater
indifferent to its destruction,
a tornado whirling *their* good air.

When the world ends,
I'll be the earthquake
that shakes up
where Privilege lives.

POINT BLANK

On summer vacation, we were black boys
playing cowboys and Indians
in a house that creaked
when we rode up warped wooden stairs.
Our imaginary horses stood and screamed.

We galloped around an antique coffee table
and claw-footed chairs in the living room—
pow, pow, your finger shot
'til you picked up your dad's gun.

At twelve, our voices started tuning themselves
and a sour scent lingered
in what was growing in our armpits.

Our teenage years were the frontier
where we battled each other
before calling time-out
for grilled cheese sandwiches
and orange Kool-Aid drink boxes.

We smiled, rubbing our faces, wondering
if our itchy chins and upper lips meant
we'd soon be our dads in the mirror,
shaving cream masking our stubbly faces.

You said the itch tingled like the aftershave
you found, searching through your father's things.
Got something to show you, you said, laughing
when I yelled: *Don't point it at me!*

You held his semiautomatic with both hands,
aiming at imaginary enemies—*pow, pow.*

And I saw that day two weeks before.
My friends, Tyler and Earl, ballers
walking from the courts,

dribbling between their legs
before some older guys
started arguing.

Idleness and Carelessness
flashed their guns at each other
before the crossfire and a ball bouncing
by two dead bodies.

I took cover behind the couch.
Sometimes I got close enough to chop your wrist
and punch your ribs.

I heard the knocking sound in my heart
and looked around the room
at the leather cranberry chaise,
chai-colored walls and the chandelier
hanging from the second floor ceiling.

I thought of mom at work,
and she became my slain friends' mothers—
baby photos across her lap,
crying every time she passed my bedroom.

I wanted to be her little boy again,
the one who held her hand to cross the street,
the one who wrestled with his dad
and ran through sprinklers in swimming trunks.

I was a boy whose world was Cap'n Crunch
and X-Men cartoons.

I wanted to go back
to my brother and me in the yard,
karate chopping invisible villains,

that age of make-believe
before the hair and body odor,
before the truth found me.

THE BLOW

I was at home lying in bed,
listening to the world wake around me:
a woman yelled from the street,
I'm gone fuck you up.

She and her man knuckled up.
They were undercard fighters
no one bothered watching, but me.

He threw a jab that barely missed.
And I thought about that day
at recess: I slapped Nicole, thinking
it was the only way she'd chase me
like she did the popular boys. In fifth grade,
she was taller than me
with a body like the women
in my mother's church,
the ones whose juicy curves
made my brain bright as a Lemonhead.

I watched the match
from my window, the couple's clumsy
footwork almost tripping them up.
Bring it on! he spat.

And I can still hear Nicole
panting behind me, yelling:
I'ma punch your face!

A week before the chase,
we were in Kevin's room
talking about the girls at school—
which one's tongue we'd let
tango across our own.
And which one's legs
we'd gladly nibble along.
My nerves fizzed like Pop Rocks

in Nicole's mouth.
My boys laughed
when her name came up.
Kevin said, *Good luck
trying to get her attention.*

The boxers outside
were still at it—she dodged his jabs.
Her right hook slammed his jaw.

God damn it! he yelled
and the fight was over.

I watched him hold his jaw,
and recalled how my ego took a blow
when I saw Nicole
hanging with a boy too cool
to wear his pants on his waist.

This is the cost of not saying
what I felt. I should've told Nicole,
after catching her scent in the hall
before lunch, I'll never think
of strawberry Bubblicious the same.

I should've made her laugh,
joking 'bout the gym teacher—
Hulk Hogan's look-alike with black hair—
or offer her some of my spicy fries.

I wish I hadn't made her
a cyclone of curses and punches
spiraling towards me.

PHANTOM PUNCH

He was Calvin, the class "comedian"
always snapping on someone: *Ey!*
Why my man's clothes look donated!

Those high school days
were chocolate Eddie Bauer jackets
and sugar cookie Timbs
dressing the Gingerbread men
women wasted their times chasing.

And you were a 10th grader
with braces and a learner's permit,
eager to jump behind the wheel and floor it
as if your life was a sports car
your parents kept in the slow lane.

Too slow for Vanessa, whose curves shouted
through tight jeans and short t-shirts.
Her walk was a pocket watch swung
from a hypnotist's fingers. Her strawberry-
glossed lips and lavender scent lingered
until getting her attention smoldered in you
like a weak barrel fire.

And you sizzled for the speed of fellas
old enough to stay out late
and buy their own clothes—
guys whose fresh Sean Jean hoodies
and Rocawear jeans said
they didn't need permission
for anything.

The bright swoosh on your Nikes—
a signature from Nee-kay, the winged
goddess of speed—was as fast
as your parents let you go.

You and your boys watched Vanessa
after a bomb threat chased everyone
from class to the parking lot.

And there was Calvin
prowling through the crowd,
looking for prey. He rocked
the red and white Jordans—
kept speckless with a toothbrush.

Vanessa thought it was cool
he didn't wear the same pair twice
in one week.

And you go back to a day in class
when he and another kid sparred—
their jokes were blows
below the belt:

Yo, your hair so nappy,
it look like chocolate covered Nerds.

But dawg, why your 'fro
look like a bowl of taco meat!

You saw Vanessa laugh
and call Calvin a fool
before you jumped in and said
Calvin couldn't get rid of his widow's peak
even if he bikini waxed his forehead.

He said you had on referee shoes—
your inky Nikes.

You looked up from the blacktop
to see Calvin smiling at you.

Ey referee, you gon' get fired
you keep showin' up

without the rest of your uniform.

Your boys dissolved into the crowd
that looped you like a noose.
Vanessa's laugh was alcohol
on a wound his words opened
when they right-hooked you.

And it stung when Calvin said
he saw you on TV running down the court.
Where your whistle at, referee?

I don't know, you said, *but if I had it,*
you'd get a technical for your shape-up.
Vanessa laughed.

TO THE WOMAN ON K STREET

He is gum pulling at your
Fendi sandal heels, a car horn's solo
in lunch time traffic. He's chased you
for blocks, knows better than to touch you.

His words barely catch up
to big hips booming
your Burberry dress like bass
in a speaker box.

You could be the kind of girl
whose city dreams
were too big for the small town
you left and never looked back.

He saw you at a traffic light,
reaching for lip gloss
when a fifty dollar bill jumped
out your bag.

You looked when he said,
Excuse me. His Timbs
told you not to look too long.

He's every man you've seen
posted up somewhere with his boys—
guys who depreciate the value
of everything around them.

That's when *you dropped something*
became *can I call you?*

You mistake him for a shoeshine man's
rag when you snapped your head away.
He is vomit on a sidewalk
that hasn't been hosed down.

You are someone who probably
grew up an ugly duckling and,
after watching fellas spoil the beautiful girls
with expensive gifts, knew you were ready
for finer things.

DON'T TELL ME

you wouldn't have done it, that you
wouldn't have taken that money. S'pose you
grew up broke. S'pose you had a childhood
being teased for wearing hand-me-downs:
Dresses so tight when you put 'em on
they could be snakes swallowing a whole animal.
S'pose you had one of those dresses on and was overtaken
by a swarm of whispers—people pointing and laughing,
sayin' you wearin' a blood pressure cuff;
people telling you your weave stink,
that you look like aunt Jemima
when you sweat. Let you have people sayin'
you won't freeze 'causa the whale blubber
keepin' you warm. Let you go through all that,
then tell me you wouldn't have lifted your bra
on a dare, that you wouldn't have done it
to see everyone on the restaurant balcony slack-jawed
over the tray of fancy cheeses and fruit platter.
Tell me you wouldn't take the opportunity
to gather up every insult and shove it back
with a smile. Tell me you wouldn't take
that hundred dollar bill on principle.
Come on. I dare you.

STRIPTEASE
for Tayib

Target's camera footage sends
security guards rushing our nephew
as he leaves the register
before they lug him to a back room.

They mistake him for a thief
returning stolen clothes for cash.
Never mind the blouse he brought back
was his mom's, that she couldn't find the receipt
and the worst she thought would happen
was a cashier saying,
Please come back when you find it.

But they're holding him for us to take home.
The store closes in twenty minutes.
Then he'll be cuffed and bounced
to a detention center.

He tells us this
through my wife's cell phone
that rang while we were cruising
to a dim restaurant, where curry
and basmati rice
fly their fragrant kites.

Our tongues tingled, thinking
of vegetable samosas—
pyramids of peas and potatoes in fried dough—
drizzled with tamarind chutney
and cilantro sauce.

But the appetites vanish
in the U-Turn. We get there
to hear the chief of security:
*What kind of mother gets her son
mixed up in her drama?*

I want to punch this black man,
but the badges and guns say it's a bad idea.
Our nephew flinches at every heavy eye
thinking they know his type,

as if his story wasn't tied to that boy,
twenty years before, browsing a store aisle, sporting
his t-shirt and jeans he bought the week before,
the ones security thought he stole
before they ripped them off him.

I'm sick of this striptease
we're forced to perform when Authority
smacks us back in line for thinking
we're like everyone else.

I'm sick of the obsession with dark skin,
the desire to see it locked down
or scoring endorsements. Our nephew knows,
at 17 and 6 feet, he'll always *fit the description*,

that his skin will justify random traffic stops—
badges cuffing him, slamming his head
into car hoods. That same skin says,
The incident at Target
is them popping his cherry.

JUST CHILLIN', B

The hours are large bills
spilling from a fat wallet.
No work today and

the lady's away.
Idleness winks at Silence.
You guys on a porch

playing dominoes or cards.
Idleness puts an arm over

your shoulder like,
Whatchall tryna' do?
Even a tree shrugs

at the wobbly question
formed by blue jays.

Time burns a hole
in your pockets.

Possibility rolls up in an Escalade.
Stereo blasting Raekwon's
"Only Built 4 Cuban Linx."

Sun smiles in the metal
and slides its light the way
a young man runs his hand
along the curves,
admiring the candy paint.

Yo, Possibility yells. *What's good!*
And y'all just grin, time facedown
like cards on the table.

ACKNOWLEDGMENTS

Grateful acknowledgment is made to the publishers and editors of the following publications where these poems previously appeared, some in slightly different form:

Boiler Journal, The: "Slippery"

Borderline (Vol. 2, Issue 7, 2012): "Getting a Little on the Side" (published as "Surveillance")

Cabildo Quarterly: "The Brute" and "Beholden"

Delaware Poetry Review: "No Substitute" and "Mr. On Time"

Dismantle: An Anthology of Writing from the VONA/ Voices Writers Workshop (Thread Makes Blanket Press, 2013): "Bloom," "Dreams of Comic Book Women," and "Sure, You Can Ask Me About Hip Hop"

Drawn to Marvel: Poems from the Comic Books (Minor Arcana Press, 2014): "X-Men" and "Dreams of Comic Book Women"

Fledgling Rag: "The Hostess" and "Freeze"

Generations: A Journal of Ideas & Images (Issue Four, Rites of Passage, Summer 2012): "Last Night at the Club" and "Phantom Punch"

Liberated Muse Volume II: Betrayal Wears A Pretty Face edited by Khadijah Z. Ali-Coleman (Liberated Muse Publication, 2012): "Hulk," "Disturbance," "The Delights," and "Exodus"

Little Patuxent Review (Issue 11, Social Justice Issue, 2012): "The Champ"

The Meadow 2011 Literary Art Journal: "Where They Do That At?"

Mixed Fruit Magazine (Issue 1, 2011): "I wanted bananas—" (published as "Bananas")

Mobius: The Journal of Social Change (Fall 2011 issue): "X-Men"

No Tell Motel (www.notellmotel.org): "Sugar Shack"

PLUCK!: "Point Blank" and "Booth Seat"

Stonecoast Review: "Swarm" and "The Angel Speaks to the New York Times"

Tak'til (taktil.webs.com): "Inner Weather"

Vinyl Poetry: "Match Sticks" and "The Exchange"

Thanks to the Stonecoast MFA program at the University of Southern Maine and to my teachers, Joy Harjo and Tim Seibles, who helped shape these poems and this collection.

Thanks to my wife, Tosin, for her honest perspectives, understanding, and patience.

Thank you, God, for our daughter, Jazmyn—who, as Joy puts it, "is my best poem." (Jaz, you're in the next collection.)

Thanks to Ewholomeyovwi Jeroro for the beautiful cover photo.

Thanks to Melanie Henderson for the author photo.

Thanks to Joseph Ross and Hayes Davis for their careful eyes.

Thanks to my best friend, brother and Jaz's godfather—
Derrick Weston Brown—for his ear and honest critiques.

Thanks to Annie Finch, Kyle Dargan, francine j. harris,
and Patricia Smith for the encouraging words.

Thanks to Tara Masih, Truth Thomas, Curtis L. Crisler,
Cedric Tillman, Barrett Warner, Sheree Renee Thomas,
and others who encouraged me to keep going until I
found a willing press.

ABOUT THE AUTHOR

Alan King is a Caribbean American, whose parents emigrated from Trinidad and Tobago to the U.S. in the 1970s. He's a husband, father, and communications professional who blogs about art and social issues at alanwking.com. A Cave Canem graduate fellow, he holds a Masters of Fine Arts in Creative Writing from the Stonecoast Program at the University of Southern Maine. He's a two-time Pushcart Prize nominee and was nominated three times for a Best of the Net selection. He lives with his family in Bowie, Maryland.

CPSIA information can be obtained
at www.ICGtesting.com
Printed in the USA
LVOW13s2301120417
530640LV00006B/435/P